JONAH

SECRET CHURCH

ISBN 979-8-9855655-2-2

Published by Radical, Inc.

Why Jonah?

Jonah is a literary masterpiece that has inspired authors, painters, poets, and musicians. But far from being some fairy tale about a fish, it's a real story with surprising relevance for our lives and the world we're living in right now. Together we will dive deep into this book.

Table of Contents ──────────────────────────

About David Platt

David Platt serves as a pastor in metro Washington, D.C. He is the founder of Radical.

David received his Ph.D. from New Orleans Baptist Theological Seminary and is the author of *Don't Hold Back, Radical, Follow Me, Counter Culture, Something Needs to Change, Before You Vote,* as well as the multiple volumes of the *Christ-Centered Exposition Commentary* series.

Along with his wife and children, he lives in the Washington, D.C., metro area.

About Radical

Jesus calls us to make his glory known among all the nations by making disciples and multiplying churches. Being on mission is not a program, but the calling of our lives as Christians.

However, 3.2 billion people are currently unreached with the gospel, and many of them endure unimaginable suffering. And, only 1% of missions dollars and 3% of missionaries go to the unreached. Something has to change.

Radical exists to equip Christians to be on mission.

RADICAL TRAINING

Radical's training program will immerse participants in the local culture while receiving biblical training from scholars and experienced global workers in the areas of church planting, evangelism, and discipleship among hard to reach people and places.

radical.net/training

RADICAL
.NET

Articles, messages, videos, Secret Church archives, podcasts, books, and many other resources to help develop mature Christians.

Visit us today!

Make Christ Known Among The Unreached

♥ give today   urgentneeds.org    URGENT

NEIGHBORHOODS & NATIONS

STORIES OF GOD'S WORK AROUND THE WORLD

▶ YOUTUBE.COM/@FOLLOWRADICAL

A book that challenges Christians to break free from

an American gospel that prioritizes comfort, power,

prosperity, and politics – and to pursue the full

beauty of the gospel of Jesus instead.

Order now

dontholdbackbook.com

DON'T HOLD BACK

LEAVING BEHIND THE AMERICAN GOSPEL TO FOLLOW *JESUS FULLY*

DAVID PLATT

NEW YORK TIMES BESTSELLING AUTHOR OF *RADICAL*

Explore Twenty Two Other Secret Church Events

Stream video, download study guides and answer keys, transcripts, discussion guides, and more all for free!

radical.net/secret-church-events

2006
2007
2008
2009
2010
2011
2012
2013
2014
2015
2016
2017
2018
2019
2020
2021
2022 $\longrightarrow$

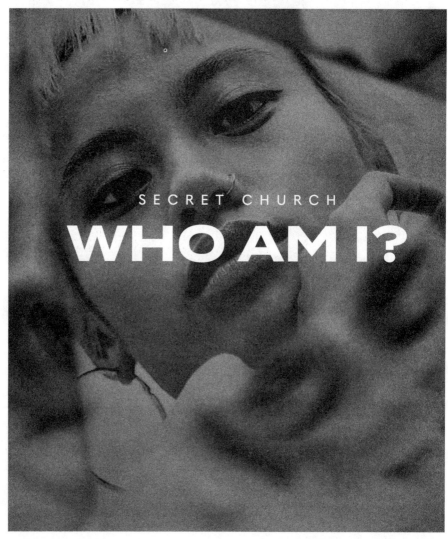

Tonight Your Generosity Can Fuel Gospel Growth in Red Zones.

Join 50,000 believers gathered this evening and give to support the most urgent physical and spiritual needs of our brothers and sisters in Iran, Yemen, Morocco, North Korea, and other persecuted places.

Radical.net/SCGive

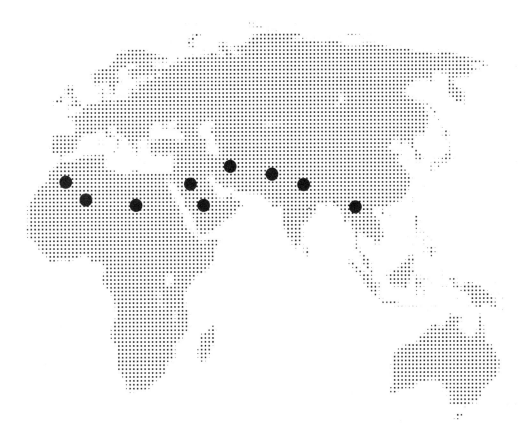

JONAH FLEES THE PRESENCE OF THE LORD

Psalm 119:162

[162] I rejoice at your word

like one who finds great spoil.

Jonah 1:1

[1] Now the word of the LORD came to Jonah

the son of Amittai, saying,

Haggai 1:1

[1] In the second year of Darius the king, in the sixth

month, on the first day of the month, the word of

the LORD came by the hand of Haggai the prophet to

Zerubbabel the son of Shealtiel, governor of Judah,

and to Joshua the son of Jehozadak, the high priest:

2 Kings 14:23-27

²³ In the fifteenth year of Amaziah the son of Joash, king

of Judah, Jeroboam the son of Joash, king of Israel, began

to reign in Samaria, and he reigned forty-one years.

²⁴ And he did what was evil in the sight of the Lord.

He did not depart from all the sins of Jeroboam the son

of Nebat, which he made Israel to sin. ²⁵ He restored the

border of Israel from Lebo-hamath as far as the Sea of

the Arabah, according to the word of the Lord, the God

of Israel, which he spoke by his servant Jonah the son

of Amittai, the prophet, who was from Gath-hepher.

2 Kings 14:23-27

[26] For the LORD saw that the affliction of Israel was very bitter, for there was none left, bond or free, and there was none to help Israel. [27] But the LORD had not said that he would blot out the name of Israel from under heaven, so he saved them by the hand of Jeroboam the son of Joash.

Hosea 7:3

[3] By their evil they make the king glad, and the princes by their treachery.

Hosea 13:10-11

[10] Where now is your king, to save you in all your cities? Where are all your rulers—those of whom you said, "Give me a king and princes"? [11] I gave you a king in my anger, and I took him away in my wrath.

Amos 7:8b-9

⁸ Then the LORD said, "Behold, I am setting a plumb line in the midst of my people Israel; I will never again pass by them; ⁹ the high places of Isaac shall be made desolate, and the sanctuaries of Israel shall be laid waste, and I will rise against the house of Jeroboam with the sword."

Amos 7:12-13

¹² And Amaziah said to Amos, "O seer, go, flee away to the land of Judah, and eat bread there, and prophesy there, ¹³ but never again prophesy at Bethel, for it is the king's sanctuary, and it is a temple of the kingdom."

2 Kings 14:25-27

²⁵ He restored the border of Israel from Lebo-hamath as far as the Sea of the Arabah, according to the word of the Lord, the God of Israel, which he spoke by his servant Jonah the son of Amittai, the prophet, who was from Gath-hepher. ²⁶ For the Lord saw that the affliction of Israel was very bitter, for there was none left, bond or free, and there was none to help Israel. ²⁷ But the Lord had not said that he would blot out the name of Israel from under heaven, so he saved them by the hand of Jeroboam the son of Joash.

Nahum 2:12

¹² The lion tore enough for his cubs and strangled prey for his lionesses; he filled his caves with prey and his dens with torn flesh.

Jonah 1:1-2

¹ Now the word of the LORD came to Jonah the

son of Amittai, saying, ² "Arise, go to Nineveh,

that great city, and call out against it, for their

evil has come up before me."

1 Kings 17:8-10

⁸ Then the word of the LORD came to him, ⁹ "Arise, go

to Zarephath, which belongs to Sidon, and dwell there.

Behold, I have commanded a widow there to feed you."

¹⁰ So he arose and went to Zarephath.

Jeremiah 13:6-7a

⁶ And after many days the LORD said to me, "Arise, go to

the Euphrates, and take from there the loincloth that

I commanded you to hide there." ⁷ Then I went to the

Euphrates,

Genesis 10:8-11a

[8] Cush fathered Nimrod; he was the first on earth to be a mighty man. [9] He was a mighty hunter before the LORD. Therefore it is said, "Like Nimrod a mighty hunter before the LORD." [10] The beginning of his kingdom was Babel, Erech, Accad, and Calneh, in the land of Shinar. [11] From that land he went into Assyria and built Nineveh,

Jonah 1:3

[3] But Jonah rose to flee to Tarshish from the presence of the LORD. He went down to Joppa and found a ship going to Tarshish. So he paid the fare and went down into it, to go with them to Tarshish, away from the presence of the LORD.

Amos 3:8

⁸ The lion has roared; who will not fear? The Lᴏʀᴅ God

has spoken; who can but prophesy?

Isaiah 66:19

¹⁹ And from them I will send survivors to the nations, to Tarshish, Pul, and Lud, who draw the bow, to Tubal and Javan, to the coastlands far away, that have not heard my fame or seen my glory.

Jonah 1:4-5a

⁴ But the LORD hurled a great wind upon the sea, and there was a mighty tempest on the sea, so that the ship threatened to break up. ⁵ Then the mariners were afraid, and each cried out to his god. And they hurled the cargo that was in the ship into the sea to lighten it for them.

Jonah 1:5b

But Jonah had gone down into the inner part of the ship and had lain down and was fast asleep.

Isaiah 14:15

[15] But you are brought down to Sheol, to the far reaches of the pit.

Genesis 15:12

[12] As the sun was going down, a deep sleep fell on Abram. And behold, dreadful and great darkness fell upon him.

Daniel 8:18

[18] And when he had spoken to me, I fell into a deep sleep with my face to the ground. But he touched me and made me stand up.

Jonah 1:6

[6] So the captain came and said to him, "What do you mean, you sleeper? Arise, call out to your god! Perhaps the god will give a thought to us, that we may not perish."

Jonah 1:7a ◦

⁷ And they said to one another, "Come, let us cast lots, that we may know on whose account this evil has come upon us."

Acts 1:24-26

²⁴ And they prayed and said, "You, Lord, who know the hearts of all, show which one of these two you have chosen ²⁵ to take the place in this ministry and apostleship from which Judas turned aside to go to his own place." ²⁶ And they cast lots for them, and the lot fell on Matthias, and he was numbered with the eleven apostles.

Proverbs 16:33

The lot is cast into the lap, but its every decision is from the LORD.

Jonah 1:7b-10a

So they cast lots, and the lot fell on Jonah. [8] Then they said to him, "Tell us on whose account this evil has come upon us. What is your occupation? And where do you come from? What is your country? And of what people are you?" [9] And he said to them, "I am a Hebrew, and I fear the Lord, the God of heaven, who made the sea and the dry land." [10] Then the men were exceedingly afraid and said to him, "What is this that you have done!"

Genesis 3:13

[13] Then the Lord God said to the woman, "What is this that you have done?"

Jonah 1:10b-14

For the men knew that he was fleeing from the presence of the Lord, because he had told them.

¹¹ Then they said to him, "What shall we do to you, that the sea may quiet down for us?" For the sea grew more and more tempestuous. ¹² He said to them, "Pick me up and hurl me into the sea; then the sea will quiet down for you, for I know it is because of me that this great tempest has come upon you." ¹³ Nevertheless, the men rowed hard to get back to dry land, but they could not, for the sea grew more and more tempestuous against them.

¹⁴ Therefore they called out to the Lord, "O Lord, let us not perish for this man's life, and lay not on us innocent blood, for you, O Lord, have done as it pleased you."

Psalm 115:3-8

3   Our God is in the heavens;

he does all that he pleases.

4   Their idols are silver and gold,

the work of human hands.

5   They have mouths, but do not speak;

eyes, but do not see.

6   They have ears, but do not hear;

noses, but do not smell.

7   They have hands, but do not feel;

feet, but do not walk;

and they do not make a sound in their throat.

8   Those who make them become like them;

so do all who trust in them.

Psalm 135:5-7

5   For I know that the LORD is great,

    and that our LORD is above all gods.

6   Whatever the LORD pleases, he does,

    in heaven and on earth,

    in the seas and all deeps.

7   He it is who makes the clouds rise at the end of

    the earth,who makes lightnings for the rain

    and brings forth the wind from his storehouses.

Isaiah 46:8-11

[8] "Remember this and stand firm, recall it to mind, you transgressors, [9] remember the former things of old; for I am God, and there is no other; I am God, and there is none like me, [10] declaring the end from the beginning and from ancient times things not yet done, saying, 'My counsel shall stand, and I will accomplish all my purpose,' [11] calling a bird of prey from the east, the man of my counsel from a far country. I have spoken, and I will bring it to pass; I have purposed, and I will do it.

Jonah 1:15-16

[15] So they picked up Jonah and hurled him into the sea, and the sea ceased from its raging.

[16] Then the men feared the LORD exceedingly, and they offered a sacrifice to the LORD and made vows.

Mark 4:41

⁴¹ And they were filled with great fear and said to one

another, "Who then is this, that even the wind and the

sea obey him?"

TAKEAWAYS

WHAT WE LEARN ABOUT GOD

- His Word is _____.

- His sovereignty is _____.

Psalm 147:8-9

8 He covers the heavens with clouds;

   he prepares rain for the earth;

   he makes grass grow on the hills.

9 He gives to the beasts their food,

   and to the young ravens that cry.

Psalm 147:16-18

16 He gives snow like wool;

   he scatters frost like ashes.

17 He hurls down his crystals of ice like crumbs;

   who can stand before his cold?

18 He sends out his word, and melts them;

   he makes his wind blow and the waters flow

- His _____ is real.

- His _____ is relentless.

WHAT WE LEARN ABOUT US

- We are inclined to_____ against God.

- We run from God's Word in _____ lives.

- We run from proclaiming God's Word

  in _____ lives.

- Our sin inevitably takes us on a downward path

  toward _____.

- It is possible for us to ground our identity in

  how the _____ defines us instead

  of how God's Word defines us.

- It is possible for us to have a kind of _____

  in God without having true _____ of God.

WHAT WE LEARN ABOUT THE WORLD

• God will draw the _____ to know

and worship him.

Psalm 46:10

10 "Be still, and know that I am God.

I will be exalted among the nations,

I will be exalted in the earth!"

Revelation 7:9-10

9 After this I looked, and behold, a great multitude

that no one could number, from every nation, from all

tribes and peoples and languages, standing before the

throne and before the Lamb, clothed in white robes,

with palm branches in their hands, 10 and crying out

with a loud voice, "Salvation belongs to our God who

sits on the throne, and to the Lamb!"

- God is not just intent on the accomplishment

  of his purpose; he is also intent on the hearts

  of his _____.

PRAYER MOMENT

SPIRITUAL AND PHYSICAL NEEDS IN IRAN

- For healthy churches to be planted among Persians throughout the region and for sound theology to take root in currently unhealthy churches.

- For the people of Iran to be open to the gospel, as sin and oppression from Islam are causing people's hearts to be closed to all religion.

- For the gospel to spread throughout the villages of Iran—beyond large cities—to unreached people groups like the Kurds, the Qashqai, and the Baloch.

- For believers to understand the importance of gathering with other believers as a church body.

- For the over 56.6 million Persians worldwide to hear the gospel. Currently, 94 of the 97 Persian people groups are classified as "unreached."

- For opportunities for Persians to hear the true gospel through multimedia projects (as possessing or distributing printed Christian material in Farsi and evangelizing are illegal) and to engage with believers through follow up.

- For indigenous Christian leaders to be trained and equipped to rise up, make disciples, and plant healthy churches.

- For God to break down strongholds and bring spiritual revival to Iran.

- For the people of Iran to encounter the ultimate freedom that comes from faith in Christ, whether the current regime folds or remains.

- For believers around the world to pray and give of their resources so that the people of Iran will be reached with the gospel.

- For government leaders to pursue justice for the people and to work against human rights abuses.

- For provision for and deliverance of Iranians suffering from poverty, drug addiction, and depression.

- For safety and protection for the vulnerable, who are often oppressed and abused.

- For all Iranians to have access to meet their basic needs.

- For God to bring justice to those who do harm to the Iranian people.

- For justice to be done amidst a rise in imprisonment and execution orders, as a result of social unrest.

Give Today♥

Support work in Iran, North Korea, Yemen, Syria, and other persecuted places

Radical.net/**SCGive**

JONAH'S PRAYER

Jonah 1:17

[17] And the LORD appointed a great fish to swallow up Jonah. And Jonah was in the belly of the fish three days and three nights.

Psalm 21:8-9

[8]   Your hand will find out all your enemies;

your right hand will find out those who hate you.

[9]   You will make them as a blazing oven

when you appear.

The LORD will swallow them up in his wrath,

and fire will consume them.

Deuteronomy 4:26-31

²⁶ I call heaven and earth to witness against you today,

that you will soon utterly perish from the land that you

are going over the Jordan to possess. You will not live

long in it, but will be utterly destroyed. ²⁷ And the LORD

will scatter you among the peoples, and you will be left

few in number among the nations where the LORD will

drive you. ²⁸ And there you will serve gods of wood and

stone, the work of human hands, that neither see, nor

hear, nor eat, nor smell. ²⁹ But from there you will seek

the LORD your God and you will find him, if you search

after him with all your heart and with all your soul.

³⁰ When you are in tribulation, and all these things come upon you in the latter days, you will return to the LORD your God and obey his voice. ³¹ For the LORD your God is a merciful God. He will not leave you or destroy you or forget the covenant with your fathers that he swore to them.

Hosea 6:1-2

¹ "Come, let us return to the LORD; for he has torn us, that he may heal us; he has struck us down, and he will bind us up. ² After two days he will revive us; on the third day he will raise us up, that we may live before him.

Jonah 2:1-2a

¹ Then Jonah prayed to the LORD his God from the belly of the fish, ² saying,

"I called out to the LORD, out of my distress, and he answered me;

Psalm 18:6

6 In my distress I called upon the LORD;

   to my God I cried for help.

   From his temple he heard my voice,

   and my cry to him reached his ears.

Psalm 120:1

1 In my distress I called to the LORD,

   and he answered me.

Jonah 2:2b

   out of the belly of Sheol I cried,

   and you heard my voice.

Job 7:9

9 As the cloud fades and vanishes, so he who goes down

to Sheol does not come up;

Isaiah 38:18

[18] For Sheol does not thank you; death does not praise

you; those who go down to the pit do not hope for your

faithfulness.

Jonah 2:3

[3]   For you cast me into the deep,

into the heart of the seas,

and the flood surrounded me;

all your waves and your billows

passed over me.

Psalm 42:7

[7]   Deep calls to deep

at the roar of your waterfalls;

all your breakers and your waves

have gone over me.

Jonah 2:4

⁴   Then I said, 'I am driven away

from your sight;

yet I shall again look

upon your holy temple.'

Genesis 3:24

²⁴ He drove out the man, and at the east of the garden

of Eden he placed the cherubim and a flaming sword

that turned every way to guard the way to the tree of

life.

Jonah 2:5-6

⁵ The waters closed in over me to take my life;

the deep surrounded me;

weeds were wrapped about my head

⁶ at the roots of the mountains.

I went down to the land

whose bars closed upon me forever;

yet you brought up my life from the pit,

O Lᴏʀᴅ my God.

Amos 2:10a

¹⁰ Also it was I who brought you up out of the land of

Egypt

Jonah 2:7-10

7   When my life was fainting away,

I remembered the Lord,

and my prayer came to you,

into your holy temple.

8   Those who pay regard to vain idols

forsake their hope of steadfast love.

9   But I with the voice of thanksgiving

will sacrifice to you;

what I have vowed I will pay.

Salvation belongs to the Lord!"

10 And the Lord spoke to the fish, and it vomited

Jonah out upon the dry land.

Psalm 32:5

5 I acknowledged my sin to you,

and I did not cover my iniquity;

I said, "I will confess my transgressions to the Lord,"

and you forgave the iniquity of my sin.

Psalm 51:1-4

1 Have mercy on me, O God,

according to your steadfast love;

according to your abundant mercy

blot out my transgressions.

2 Wash me thoroughly from my iniquity,

and cleanse me from my sin!

3 For I know my transgressions,

and my sin is ever before me.

4 Against you, you only, have I sinned

and done what is evil in your sight,

so that you may be justified in your words

and blameless in your judgment.

Jonah 2:2-9

2 "I called out to the LORD, out of my distress,

and he answered me;

out of the belly of Sheol I cried,

and you heard my voice.

3 For you cast me into the deep,

into the heart of the seas,

and the flood surrounded me;

all your waves and your billows

passed over me.

4   Then I said, 'I am driven away

      from your sight;

      yet I shall again look

      upon your holy temple.'

5   The waters closed in over me to take my life;

      the deep surrounded me;

weeds were wrapped about my head

6   at the roots of the mountains.

I went down to the land

      whose bars closed upon me forever;

yet you brought up my life from the pit,

O Lord my God.

7   When my life was fainting away,

      I remembered the Lord,

and my prayer came to you,

      into your holy temple.

8   Those who pay regard to vain idols

     forsake their hope of steadfast love.

9   But I with the voice of thanksgiving

     will sacrifice to you;

   what I have vowed I will pay.

     Salvation belongs to the Lord!"

Genesis 8:1

8 But God remembered Noah and all the beasts and all the livestock that were with him in the ark. And God made a wind blow over the earth, and the waters subsided.

Luke 18:11-13

[11] The Pharisee, standing by himself, prayedthus: 'God, I thank you that I am not like other men, extortioners, unjust, adulterers, or even like this tax collector. [12] I fast twice a week; I give tithes of all that I get.' [13] But the tax collector, standing far off, would not even lift up his eyes to heaven, but beat his breast, saying, 'God, be merciful to me, a sinner!'

1 Samuel 15:22-23

[22] And Samuel said, "Has the LORD as great delight in burnt offerings and sacrifices, as in obeying the voice of the LORD? Behold, to obey is better than sacrifice, and to listen than the fat of rams. [23] For rebellion is as the sin of divination, and presumption is as iniquity and idolatry."

TAKEAWAYS

- God is merciful toward the most

  _____ sinners.

- God is able to bring life to the _____.

Matthew 12:38-40

[38] Then some of the scribes and Pharisees answered him,

saying, "Teacher, we wish to see a sign from you." [39] But

he answered them, "An evil and adulterous generation

seeks for a sign, but no sign will be given to it except the

sign of the prophet Jonah. [40] For just as Jonah was three

days and three nights in the belly of the great fish, so

will the Son of Man be three days and three nights in the

heart of the earth.

- Jonah experienced judgment for _____ sin.

- Jesus experienced judgment for _____ sin.

- Jonah was alive after three days in a _____.

- Jesus was alive after three days in a _____.

Jonah 2:6

6   at the roots of the mountains.

I went down to the land

whose bars closed upon me forever;

yet you brought up my life from the pit,

O LORD my God.

Genesis 50:20

20 As for you, you meant evil against me, but God meant

it for good, to bring it about that many people should be

kept alive, as they are today.

Psalm 49:14-15

14 Like sheep they are appointed for Sheol;

    death shall be their shepherd,

and the upright shall rule over them in the morning.

    Their form shall be consumed in Sheol, with

      no place to dwell.

15 But God will ransom my soul from the power of Sheol,

    for he will receive me.

Psalm 73:26

26 My flesh and my heart may fail,

    but God is the strength of my heart and my portion

forever.

Matthew 19:26

²⁶ But Jesus looked at them and said, "With man this is impossible, but with God all things are possible."

Romans 5:7-8

⁷ For one will scarcely die for a righteous person—though perhaps for a good person one would dare even to die—⁸ but God shows his love for us in that while we were still sinners, Christ died for us.

Romans 6:23

²³ For the wages of sin is death, but the free gift of God is eternal life in Christ Jesus our Lord.

● ● ●

Ephesians 2:1-9

¹ And you were dead in the trespasses and sins ² in which you once walked, following the course of this world, following the prince of the power of the air, the spirit that is now at work in the sons of disobedience—

³ among whom we all once lived in the passions of our flesh, carrying out the desires of the body and the mind, and were by nature children of wrath, like the rest of mankind. ⁴ But God, being rich in mercy, because of the great love with which he loved us,

[5] even when we were dead in our trespasses, made us alive together with Christ—by grace you have been saved— [6] and raised us up with him and seated us with him in the heavenly places in Christ Jesus, [7] so that in the coming ages he might show the immeasurable riches of his grace in kindness toward us in Christ Jesus. [8] For by grace you have been saved through faith. And this is not your own doing; it is the gift of God, [9] not a result of works, so that no one may boast.

Acts 13:29-30

[29] And when they had carried out all that was written of him, they took him down from the tree and laid him in a tomb. [30] But God raised him from the dead,

- God is sovereign over all _____.

- God alone is the _____ of salvation.

Acts 4:12

[12] And there is salvation in no one else, for there is no

other name under heaven given among men by which we

must be saved."

Jonah 2:9

[9]   But I with the voice of thanksgiving

   will sacrifice to you;

what I have vowed I will pay.

   Salvation belongs to the Lord!"

Matthew 1:21

[21] She will bear a son, and you shall call his name Jesus, for

he will save his people from their sins."

- God alone is the _____ of salvation.

Exodus 33:19

[19] And he said, "I will make all my goodness pass before you and will proclaim before you my name 'The LORD.' And I will be gracious to whom I will be gracious, and will show mercy on whom I will show mercy."

Romans 9:16

[16] So then it depends not on human will or exertion, but on God, who has mercy.

Revelation 7:9-10

[9] After this I looked, and behold, a great multitude that no one could number, from every nation, from all tribes and peoples and languages, standing before the throne and before the Lamb, clothed in white robes, with palm branches in their hands, [10] and crying out with a loud voice, "Salvation belongs to our God who sits on the throne, and to the Lamb!"

PRAYER MOMENT

FOR THE CHURCH

- For unity among the church in Iran.

- For opportunities for Christians to experience community with other believers.

- For new believers to be able to connect with other Christians who can disciple them.

- For the safety and security of teams that are boldly ministering in and around Iran.

- For Christians in prison to have perseverance, joy, and the ability to recall Scripture.

- For the church to hope in Jesus more than a change in the government leadership.

- For the church to be wise and to faithfully share the gospel, rather than being distracted by political unrest.

- For God to protect church leaders from persecution, temptation, and sin.

- For the health of churches in Iran.

- For home churches to meet together in biblical community.

- For believers to hold fast to their faith, in the face of persecution and temptation to renounce it.

Give Today♥

Support work in Iran, North Korea, Yemen, Syria, and other persecuted places

Radical.net/**SCGive**

Session 3 | Jonah 3

JONAH GOES TO NINEVEH

Jonah 3:1

[1] Then the word of the LORD came to Jonah the

second time, saying,

Jonah 1:1

[1] Now the word of the LORD came to Jonah the

son of Amittai, saying,

Matthew 16:13-18

[13] Now when Jesus came into the district of Caesarea

Philippi, he asked his disciples, "Who do people say that

the Son of Man is?" [14] And they said, "Some say John the

Baptist, others say Elijah, and others Jeremiah or one of

the prophets." [15] He said to them, "But who do you say

that I am?" [16] Simon Peter replied, "You are the Christ, the

Son of the living God."

[17] And Jesus answered him, "Blessed are you, Simon Bar-

Jonah! For flesh and blood has not revealed this to you, but my Father who is in heaven. [18] And I tell you, you are Peter, and on this rock I will build my church, and the gates of hell shall not prevail against it.

Acts 10:5

[5] And now send men to Joppa and bring one Simon who is called Peter.

Jonah 3:2-4

[2] "Arise, go to Nineveh, that great city, and call out against it the message that I tell you." [3] So Jonah arose and went to Nineveh, according to the word of the Lord. Now Nineveh was an exceedingly great city, three days' journey in breadth. [4] Jonah began to go into the city, going a day's journey. And he called out, "Yet forty days, and Nineveh shall be overthrown!"

Genesis 6:5-7

⁵ The Lᴏʀᴅ saw that the wickedness of man was great in the earth, and that every intention of the thoughts of his heart was only evil continually. ⁶ And the Lᴏʀᴅ regretted that he had made man on the earth, and it grieved him to his heart. ⁷ So the Lᴏʀᴅ said, "I will blot out man whom I have created from the face of the land, man and animals and creeping things and birds of the heavens, for I am sorry that I have made them."

Genesis 7:17-23

¹⁷ The flood continued forty days on the earth. The waters increased and bore up the ark, and it rose high above the earth. ¹⁸ The waters prevailed and increased greatly on the earth, and the ark floated on the face of the waters. ¹⁹ And the waters prevailed so mightily on the earth that all the high mountains under the whole heaven were covered.

20 The waters prevailed above the mountains, covering them fifteen cubits deep. 21 And all flesh died that moved on the earth, birds, livestock, beasts, all swarming creatures that swarm on the earth, and all mankind. 22 Everything on the dry land in whose nostrils was the breath of life died. 23 He blotted out every living thing that was on the face of the ground, man and animals and creeping things and birds of the heavens. They were blotted out from the earth.

Deuteronomy 9:25

25 "So I lay prostrate before the LORD for these forty days and forty nights, because the LORD had said he would destroy you.

Numbers 13:25

25 At the end of forty days they returned from spying out the land.

Numbers 14:32-35

³² But as for you, your dead bodies shall fall in this wilderness. ³³ And your children shall be shepherds in the wilderness forty years and shall suffer for your faithlessness, until the last of your dead bodies lies in the wilderness. ³⁴ According to the number of the days in which you spied out the land, forty days, a year for each day, you shall bear your iniquity forty years, and you shall know my displeasure.' ³⁵ I, the LORD, have spoken. Surely this will I do to all this wicked congregation who are gathered together against me: in this wilderness they shall come to a full end, and there they shall die."

Jonah 3:4b

And he called out, "Yet forty days, and Nineveh shall be overthrown!"

Genesis 19:24-25

²⁴ Then the LORD rained on Sodom and Gomorrah sulfur and fire from the LORD out of heaven. ²⁵ And he overthrew those cities, and all the valley, and all the inhabitants of the cities, and what grew on the ground.

Esther 9:22

²² as the days on which the Jews got relief from their enemies, and as the month that had been turned for them from sorrow into gladness and from mourning into a holiday;

Jonah 3:5a

⁵ And the people of Nineveh believed God.

Genesis 15:6

⁶ And he believed the LORD, and he counted it to him as righteousness.

Jonah 3:5b

They called for a fast and put on sackcloth, from the greatest of them to the least of them.

1 Kings 21:27

27 And when Ahab heard those words, he tore his clothes and put sackcloth on his flesh and fasted and lay in sackcloth and went about dejectedly.

Daniel 9:3-4a

3 Then I turned my face to the Lord God, seeking him by prayer and pleas for mercy with fasting and sackcloth and ashes. 4 I prayed to the Lord my God and made confession,

Jonah 3:6-8a

[6] The word reached the king of Nineveh, and he arose from his throne, removed his robe, covered himself with sackcloth, and sat in ashes.

[7] And he issued a proclamation and published through Nineveh, "By the decree of the king and his nobles: Let neither man nor beast, herd nor flock, taste anything. Let them not feed or drink water, [8] but let man and beast be covered with sackcloth, and let them call out mightily to God.

Joel 1:18

[18] How the beasts groan! The herds of cattle are perplexed because there is no pasture for them; even the flocks of sheep suffer.

Joel 1:20

[20] Even the beasts of the field pant for you because the water brooks are dried up, and fire has devoured the pastures of the wilderness.

Joel 2:22

[22] Fear not, you beasts of the field, for the pastures of the wilderness are green; the tree bears its fruit; the fig tree and vine give their full yield.

Jonah 3:8b-9

Let everyone turn from his evil way and from the violence that is in his hands. [9] Who knows? God may turn and relent and turn from his fierce anger, so that we may not perish."

Joel 2:14

¹⁴ Who knows whether he will not turn and relent, and

leave a blessing behind him, a grain offering and a drink

offering for the Lord your God?

Jonah 1:6

⁶ Arise, call out to your god! Perhaps the god will

give a thought to us, that we may not perish."

Jonah 1:14a

¹⁴ Therefore they called out to the Lord, "O Lord,

let us not perish for this man's life,

Jonah 3:10

[10] When God saw what they did, how they turned from their evil way, God relented of the disaster that he had said he would do to them, and he did not do it.

Jeremiah 18:7-8

[7] If at any time I declare concerning a nation or a kingdom, that I will pluck up and break down and destroy it, [8] and if that nation, concerning which I have spoken, turns from its evil, I will relent of the disaster that I intended to do to it.

Exodus 32:14

[14] And the LORD relented from the disaster that he had spoken of bringing on his people.

Numbers 23:19

¹⁹ God is not man, that he should lie, or a son of man, that

he should change his mind. Has he said, and will he not

do it? Or has he spoken, and will he not fulfill it?

TAKEAWAYS

- _____ and _____ God's mercy!

2 Kings 17:13-15

[13] Yet the LORD warned Israel and Judah by every prophet and every seer, saying, "Turn from your evil ways and keep my commandments and my statutes, in accordance with all the Law that I commanded your fathers, and that I sent to you by my servants the prophets." [14] But they would not listen, but were stubborn, as their fathers had been, who did not believe in the LORD their God. [15] They despised his statutes and his covenant that he made with their fathers and the warnings that he gave them.

Matthew 12:38-41

[38] Then some of the scribes and Pharisees answered him, saying, "Teacher, we wish to see a sign from you." [39] But he answered them, "An evil and adulterous generation seeks for a sign, but no sign will be given to it except the sign of the prophet Jonah.

⁴⁰ For just as Jonah was three days and three nights in the belly of the great fish, so will the Son of Man be three days and three nights in the heart of the earth.

⁴¹ The men of Nineveh will rise up at the judgment with this generation and condemn it, for they repented at the preaching of Jonah, and behold, something greater than Jonah is here.

Mark 1:15b

Repent and believe in the gospel.

- _____ to repent and receive

  God's mercy!

Jonah 3:1

¹ The word of the LORD came to Jonah, saying,

"Arise, go to Nineveh, that great city, and call

out against it the message that I tell you."

Matthew 28:18-20

¹⁸ And Jesus came and said to them, "All authority in

heaven and on earth has been given to me. ¹⁹ Go therefore

and make disciples of all nations, baptizing them in the

name of the Father and of the Son and of the Holy Spirit,

²⁰ teaching them to observe all that I have commanded

you. And behold, I am with you always, to the end of the

age."

Acts 1:8

8 "But you will receive power when the Holy Spirit has come upon you, and you will be my witnesses in Jerusalem and in all Judea and Samaria, and to the end of the earth."

Acts 2:37-41

37 Now when they heard this they were cut to the heart, and said to Peter and the rest of the apostles, "Brothers, what shall we do?" 38 And Peter said to them, "Repent and be baptized every one of you in the name of Jesus Christ for the forgiveness of your sins, and you will receive the gift of the Holy Spirit. 39 For the promise is for you and for your children and for all who are far off, everyone whom the Lord our God calls to himself."

⁴⁰ And with many other words he bore witness and continued to exhort them, saying, "Save yourselves from this crooked generation." ⁴¹ So those who received his word were baptized, and there were added that day about three thousand souls.

Ezekiel 33:1-9

¹ The word of the Lᴏʀᴅ came to me: ² "Son of man, speak to your people and say to them, If I bring the sword upon a land, and the people of the land take a man from among them, and make him their watchman, ³ and if he sees the sword coming upon the land and blows the trumpet and warns the people, ⁴ then if anyone who hears the sound of the trumpet does not take warning, and the sword comes and takes him away, his blood shall be upon his own head.

⁵ He heard the sound of the trumpet and did not take warning; his blood shall be upon himself. But if he had taken warning, he would have saved his life. ⁶ But if the watchman sees the sword coming and does not blow the trumpet, so that the people are not warned, and the sword comes and takes any one of them, that person is taken away in his iniquity, but his blood I will require at the watchman's hand. ⁷ "So you, son of man, I have made a watchman for the house of Israel. Whenever you hear a word from my mouth, you shall give them warning from me. ⁸ If I say to the wicked, O wicked one, you shall surely die, and you do not speak to warn the wicked to turn from his way, that wicked person shall die in his iniquity, but his blood I will require at your hand. ⁹ But if you warn the wicked to turn from his way, and he does not turn from his way, that person shall die in his iniquity, but you will have delivered your soul.

- Trust the _____ of God's Word.

Acts 2:41

41 So those who received his word were baptized, and there were added that day about three thousand souls.

Acts 4:4

4 But many of those who had heard the word believed, and the number of the men came to about five thousand.

Acts 4:29-31

29 And now, Lord, look upon their threats and grant to your servants to continue to speak your word with all boldness, 30 while you stretch out your hand to heal, and signs and wonders are performed through the name of your holy servant Jesus." 31 And when they had prayed, the place in which they were gathered together was shaken, and they were all filled with the Holy Spirit and continued to speak the word of God with boldness.

Acts 6:4

4 "But we will devote ourselves to prayer and to the ministry of the word."

Acts 6:7a

7 And the word of God continued to increase, and the number of the disciples multiplied greatly in Jerusalem,

Acts 8:4

4 Now those who were scattered went about preaching the word.

Acts 8:14

14 Now when the apostles at Jerusalem heard that Samaria had received the word of God, they sent to them Peter and John,

Acts 8:25

25 Now when they had testified and spoken the word of the Lord, they returned to Jerusalem, preaching the gospel to many villages of the Samaritans.

Acts 10:44

44 While Peter was still saying these things, the Holy

Spirit fell on all who heard the word.

Acts 11:1

11 Now the apostles and the brothers who were

throughout Judea heard that the Gentiles also had

received the word of God.

Acts 11:19

19 Now those who were scattered because of the

persecution that arose over Stephen traveled as far as

Phoenicia and Cyprus and Antioch, speaking the word

to no one except Jews.

Acts 12:24

24 But the word of God increased and multiplied.

Acts 13:5a

5 When they arrived at Salamis, they proclaimed the

word of God in the synagogues of the Jews.

Acts 13:7

7 He was with the proconsul, Sergius Paulus, a man of intelligence, who summoned Barnabas and Saul and sought to hear the word of God.

Acts 13:44-49

44 The next Sabbath almost the whole city gathered to hear the word of the Lord. 45 But when the Jews saw the crowds, they were filled with jealousy and began to contradict what was spoken by Paul, reviling him.

46 And Paul and Barnabas spoke out boldly, saying, "It was necessary that the word of God be spoken first to you. Since you thrust it aside and judge yourselves unworthy of eternal life, behold, we are turning to the Gentiles. 47 For so the Lord has commanded us, saying,

"'I have made you a light for the Gentiles, that you may bring salvation to the ends of the earth.'"

48 And when the Gentiles heard this, they began rejoicing and glorifying the word of the Lord, and as many as were appointed to eternal life believed. 49 And the word of the Lord was spreading throughout the whole region.

Acts 14:25

25 And when they had spoken the word in Perga, they went down to Attalia,

Acts 15:35-36

35 But Paul and Barnabas remained in Antioch, teaching and preaching the word of the Lord, with many others also. 36 And after some days Paul said to Barnabas, "Let us return and visit the brothers in every city where we proclaimed the word of the Lord, and see how they are."

Acts 16:32

32 And they spoke the word of the Lord to him and to all who were in his house.

Acts 17:11

11 Now these Jews were more noble than those in

Thessalonica; they received the word with all eagerness,

examining the Scriptures daily to see if these things were

so.

Acts 18:5

5 When Silas and Timothy arrived from Macedonia, Paul

was occupied with the word, testifying to the Jews that

the Christ was Jesus.

Acts 18:11

11 And he stayed a year and six months, teaching the word

of God among them.

Acts 19:10

10 This continued for two years, so that all the residents

of Asia heard the word of the Lord, both Jews and Greeks.

Acts 19:20

20 So the word of the Lord continued to increase and

prevail mightily.

- Proclaim it all over the _____.

Matthew 9:37-38

37 Then he said to his disciples, "The harvest is plentiful,

but the laborers are few; 38 therefore pray earnestly

to the Lord of the harvest to send out laborers into his

harvest."

Jonah 3:4b

And he called out, "Yet forty days, and Nineveh

shall be overthrown!"

PRAYER MOMENT

FOR GOSPEL GROWTH & MINISTRY WORK

- For church leadership development work among Persians.

- For wide-reaching evangelism follow-up efforts to be fruitful so that the church will grow.

- For healthy churches to be planted among Persians in Iran and the surrounding region.

- For many Persians to hear the gospel through multimedia evangelism efforts.

- For protection for workers who have distributed God's Word.

- For church leaders to stand firm.

- For pastors and leaders to grow in their ability to shepherd their churches through social and political unrest.

Give Today ♥

Support work in Iran, North Korea, Yemen, Syria, and other persecuted places

Radical.net/**SCGive**

JONAH'S ANGER AND THE LORD'S COMPASSION

Jonah 3:10

10 When God saw what they did, how they turned from their evil way, God relented of the disaster that he had said he would do to them, and he did not do it.

Jonah 4:1-2a

1 But it displeased Jonah exceedingly, and he was angry. 2 And he prayed to the Lord

Jonah 2:1

[1]Then Jonah prayed to the LORD his God from

the belly of the fish,

Jonah 4:2b

and said, "O LORD, is not this what I said when

I was yet in my country? That is why I made

haste to flee to Tarshish; for I knew that you are

a gracious God and merciful, slow to anger and

abounding in steadfast love, and relenting from

disaster.

Exodus 34:6-8

6 The LORD passed before him and proclaimed, "The

LORD, the LORD, a God merciful and gracious, slow to

anger, and abounding in steadfast love and faithfulness,

7 keeping steadfast love for thousands, forgiving iniquity

and transgression and sin, but who will by no means

clear the guilty, visiting the iniquity of the fathers on the

children and the children's children, to the third and the

fourth generation." 8 And Moses quickly bowed his head

toward the earth and worshiped.

Numbers 14:18-19

18 'The LORD is slow to anger and abounding in steadfast

love, forgiving iniquity and transgression, but he will

by no means clear the guilty, visiting the iniquity of

the fathers on the children, to the third and the fourth

generation.'

Psalm 86:15

15 But you, O Lord, are a God merciful and gracious,

slow to anger and abounding in steadfast love and

faithfulness.

Psalm 103:8

8 The Lord is merciful and gracious,

slow to anger and abounding in steadfast love.

Nehemiah 9:16-17

16 "But they and our fathers acted presumptuously

and stiffened their neck and did not obey your

commandments. 17 They refused to obey and were not

mindful of the wonders that you performed among them,

but they stiffened their neck and appointed a leader to

return to their slavery in Egypt. But you are a God ready

to forgive, gracious and merciful, slow to anger and

abounding in steadfast love, and did not forsake them."

2 Kings 17:6

⁶ In the ninth year of Hoshea, the king of Assyria captured Samaria, and he carried the Israelites away to Assyria and placed them in Halah, and on the Habor, the river of Gozan, and in the cities of the Medes.

Jonah 4:3

³ Therefore now, O LORD, please take my life from me, for it is better for me to die than to live."

1 Kings 19:4

⁴ But he himself went a day's journey into the wilderness and came and sat down under a broom tree. And he asked that he might die, saying, "It is enough; now, O LORD, take away my life, for I am no better than my fathers."

Jonah 2:6b-9

you brought up my life from the pit, O LORD

my God. [7] When my life was fainting away, I

remembered the LORD, and my prayer came

to you, into your holy temple. [8] Those who

pay regard to vain idols forsake their hope

of steadfast love. [9] But I with the voice of

thanksgiving will sacrifice to you; what I have

vowed I will pay. Salvation belongs to the LORD!"

Jonah 4:4

[4] And the LORD said, "Do you do well to be

angry?"

Genesis 3:9-13

9 But the LORD God called to the man and said to him, "Where are you?" 10 And he said, "I heard the sound of you in the garden, and I was afraid, because I was naked, and I hid myself." 11 He said, "Who told you that you were naked? Have you eaten of the tree of which I commanded you not to eat?" 12 The man said, "The woman whom you gave to be with me, she gave me fruit of the tree, and I ate." 13 Then the LORD God said to the woman, "What is this that you have done?"

Genesis 4:9-10

9 Then the LORD said to Cain, "Where is Abel your brother?" He said, "I do not know; am I my brother's keeper?" 10 And the LORD said, "What have you done?"

Luke 22:48

48 Jesus said to him, "Judas, would you betray the Son of Man with a kiss?"

Job 38:1-3

1 Then the Lord answered Job out of the whirlwind and

said:

2 "Who is this that darkens counsel by words without

    knowledge?

3 Dress for action like a man;

    I will question you, and you make it known to me."

Jonah 4:5a

5 Jonah went out of the city and sat to the east of

the city and made a booth for himself there.

Genesis 3:24

24 He drove out the man, and at the east of the garden of

Eden he placed the cherubim and a flaming sword that

turned every way to guard the way to the tree of life.

Genesis 4:16

16 Then Cain went away from the presence of the LORD

and settled in the land of Nod, east of Eden.

Genesis 11:2

2 And as people migrated from the east, they found a

plain in the land of Shinar and settled there.

Genesis 13:11-13

11 So Lot chose for himself all the Jordan Valley, and Lot

journeyed east. Thus they separated from each other.

12 Abram settled in the land of Canaan, while Lot settled

among the cities of the valley and moved his tent as far

as Sodom. 13 Now the men of Sodom were wicked, great

sinners against the LORD.

Zechariah 14:16

16 Then everyone who survives of all the nations that

have come against Jerusalem shall go up year after year

to worship the King, the Lord of hosts, and to keep the

Feast of Booths.

Jonah 4:5b

He sat under it in the shade, till he should see

what would become of the city.

Exodus 32:31-32

31 "Alas, this people has sinned a great sin. They have made for themselves gods of gold. 32 But now, if you will forgive their sin—but if not, please blot me out of your book that you have written."

Jonah 4:6

6 Now the LORD God appointed a plant and made it come up over Jonah, that it might be a shade over his head, to save him from his discomfort.

Jonah 1:9

9 And he said to them, "I am a Hebrew, and I fear the LORD, the God of heaven, who made the sea and the dry land."

Jonah 2:1

¹ Then Jonah prayed to the Lord his God from

the belly of the fish,

Jonah 2:6

6   at the roots of the mountains.

I went down to the land

whose bars closed upon me forever;

yet you brought up my life from the pit,

O Lord my God.

Jonah 4:6-11

⁶ Now the Lᴏʀᴅ God appointed a plant and made it come up over Jonah, that it might be a shade over his head, to save him from his discomfort. So Jonah was exceedingly glad because of the plant. ⁷ But when dawn came up the next day, God appointed a worm that attacked the plant, so that it withered. ⁸ When the sun rose, God appointed a scorching east wind, and the sun beat down on the head of Jonah so that he was faint. And he asked that he might die and said, "It is better for me to die than to live." ⁹ But God said to Jonah, "Do you do well to be angry for the plant?" And he said, "Yes, I do well to be angry, angry enough to die."

¹⁰ And the LORD said, "You pity the plant, for which you did not labor, nor did you make it grow, which came into being in a night and perished in a night. ¹¹ And should not I pity Nineveh, that great city, in which there are more than 120,000 persons who do not know their right hand from their left, and also much cattle?"

Deuteronomy 5:32-33

³² You shall be careful therefore to do as the LORD your God has commanded you. You shall not turn aside to the right hand or to the left. ³³ You shall walk in all the way that the LORD your God has commanded you, that you may live, and that it may go well with you, and that you may live long in the land that you shall possess.

Deuteronomy 17:11

11 According to the instructions that they give you, and according to the decision which they pronounce to you, you shall do. You shall not turn aside from the verdict that they declare to you, either to the right hand or to the left.

Joshua 23:6

6 Therefore, be very strong to keep and to do all that is written in the Book of the Law of Moses, turning aside from it neither to the right hand nor to the left,

Romans 2:14-15a

14 For when Gentiles, who do not have the law, by nature do what the law requires, they are a law to themselves, even though they do not have the law. 15 They show that the work of the law is written on their hearts,

SEVEN QUESTIONS

1. Have you ever wanted (or even now, do you ever

   want) your_____ more than God's_____?

2. Are you inclined to settle for the comforts of people

   and places that are _____ to you instead

   of paying a cost to go to people and places that are

   _____ to you? (Especially if those

   people are threatening to you or perceived as your

   enemies?)

3. How often do you _____ for and desire

   the good of other people (and countries) that may

   be considered your enemies (or enemies of your

   country)?

4. Have you ever _____ (at least in

your mind) the justice of God or the mercy of God?

5. Is it possible for you to know about the character

of God yet not show the _____ of God?

6. Do you sometimes care more about your earthly

desires than others' eternal _____ ?

7. What do you truly want more: a comfortable life

in _____ nation or the spread of the gospel

in _____ nations?

TAKEAWAYS

- We are _____.

- It is possible for us to _____

  the mercy of God yet _____

  the mission of God.

  - We like our _____.

  - We lack _____ for others.

  - We don't like God's _____.

  - We don't like God's _____.

- We need _____.

- We need Jesus to _____ us from our sin

  and _____ us to live

  on mission with him.

Matthew 4:19

[19] And he said to them, "Follow me, and I will make you

fishers of men."

Matthew 28:18-20

[18] And Jesus came and said to them, "All authority in

heaven and on earth has been given to me. [19] Go therefore

and make disciples of all nations, baptizing them in the

name of the Father and of the Son and of the Holy Spirit,

[20] teaching them to observe all that I have commanded

you. And behold, I am with you always, to the end of the

age."

- We need Jesus to so transform us that when we see

  wrong and/or are wronged, we _____

  and _____ the mercy of God.

2 Peter 3:5-9

5 For they deliberately overlook this fact, that the heavens

existed long ago, and the earth was formed out of water

and through water by the word of God, 6 and that by

means of these the world that then existed was deluged

with water and perished. 7 But by the same word the

heavens and earth that now exist are stored up for fire,

being kept until the day of judgment and destruction of

the ungodly. 8 But do not overlook this one fact, beloved,

that with the Lord one day is as a thousand years, and a

thousand years as one day.

9 The Lord is not slow to fulfill his promise as some count slowness, but is patient toward you, not wishing that any should perish, but that all should reach repentance.

- We need Jesus to so transform us that when we see wrong and/or are wronged, we _____ and _____ for the justice of God.

Nahum 1:1-3

An oracle concerning Nineveh. The book of the vision of Nahum of Elkosh. 2 The LORD is a jealous and avenging God; the LORD is avenging and wrathful; the LORD takes vengeance on his adversaries and keeps wrath for his enemies. 3 The LORD is slow to anger and great in power, and the LORD will by no means clear the guilty.

Nahum 3:18-19

18 Your shepherds are asleep, O king of Assyria; your

nobles slumber. Your people are scattered on the

mountains with none to gather them. 19 There is no

easing your hurt; your wound is grievous. All who hear

the news about you clap their hands over you. For upon

whom has not come your unceasing evil?

Revelation 19:1b-2a

"Hallelujah!

Salvation and glory and power belong to our God,

2   for his judgments are true and just;

- We need Jesus to so transform us that we _____

intentionally for the good of other people (and

countries) that might be considered our

_____ (or enemies of our country).

Luke 23:34

34 And Jesus said, "Father, forgive them, for they know

not what they do."

Acts 7:60

60 And falling to his knees he cried out with a loud voice,

"Lord, do not hold this sin against them."

- We need Jesus to so transform us that we

  _____ for the spread of

  the gospel to all nations, particularly those with

  the least access to the gospel.

- We need Jesus to so transform us that we _____

  willingly and gladly for the nations right where

  we live and _____ God leads.

A FINAL WORD & QUESTION

- Your disobedience does not have to be the

  _____ of your story.

- His exaltation will be the end of _____ .

Revelation 7:9-12

9 After this I looked, and behold, a great multitude that

no one could number, from every nation, from all tribes

and peoples and languages, standing before the throne

and before the Lamb, clothed in white robes, with palm

branches in their hands, 10 and crying out with a loud

voice, "Salvation belongs to our God who sits on the

throne, and to the Lamb!"

[11] And all the angels were standing around the throne and around the elders and the four living creatures, and they fell on their faces before the throne and worshiped God, [12] saying, "Amen! Blessing and glory and wisdom and thanksgiving and honor and power and might be to our God forever and ever! Amen."

- Will your story _____ with the purpose of his story?

_____

_____

_____

_____

_____

_____

PRAYER MOMENT

FOR OUR LIVES

God, as a recipient of your grace, I will do whatever you call me to do—no matter the cost—to get the gospel to people who have never heard it.

Give Today♥

Support work in Iran, North Korea, Yemen, Syria, and other persecuted places

Radical.net/**SCGive**

Answer Key

Session 01

Page 35 - authoritative, absolute
Page 36 - wrath, mercy
Page 37 - rebel, our, others', death, world, faith, fear
Page 38 - nations
Page 39 - people

Session 02

Page 57 - undeserving, dead
Page 58 - his, our, fish, grave
Page 62 - salvation
Page 63 - author, giver

Session 03

Page 79 - Repent, receive
Page 81 - Call others
Page 86 - power
Page 92 - world

Session 04

Page 111 - way, will, familiar, foreign, pray
Page 112 - questioned, compassion, destinies, your, all
Page 113 - Jonah, receive, resist, comforts, concern, commission, character, Jesus
Page 114 - save, transform
Page 115 - remember, reflect
Page 116 - trust, wait
Page 117 - pray, enemies
Page 118 - give sacrificially, go, wherever
Page 119 - end, history
Page 120 - align

Recommended Resources

Baker, David W., T. Desmond Alexander, and Bruce K. Waltke. *Obadiah, Jonah and Micah.* Tyndale Old Testament Commentaries, ed. Donald J. Wiseman.

Bruckner, James. *Jonah, Nahum, Habakkuk, Zephaniah.* The NIV Application Commentary, ed. Terry Muck.

Estelle, Bryan D. *Salvation through Judgment and Mercy: The Gospel According to Jonah.* The Gospel According to the Old Testament, ed. Iain M. Duguid.

McComiskey, Thomas, ed. *The Minor Prophets Volume II: A Commentary on Obadiah, Jonah, Micah, Nahum, Habakkuk.*

Stuart, Douglas. *Hosea-Jonah.* World Biblical Commentary, ed. Bruce M. Metzger, David A. Hubbard, Glenn W. Barker.

Timmer, Daniel. *A Gracious and Compassionate God: Mission, Salvation and Spirituality in the Book of Jonah.* New Studies in Biblical Theology, ed. D. A. Carson.

Townsend, Cynthia. *Jonah for all the Peoples.* (Children's Book)

Youngblood, Kevin. *Jonah: A Discourse Analysis of the Hebrew Bible.* Zondervan Exegetical Commentary on the Old Testament, ed. Daniel I. Block.

Note: Not everything contained in these resources is endorsed by David Platt or Radical. As always, we encourage you to compare what you read with the teaching of Scripture, which is our ultimate authority.

Notes

Secret Church

Notes

Secret Church

APPAREL WITH PURPOSE

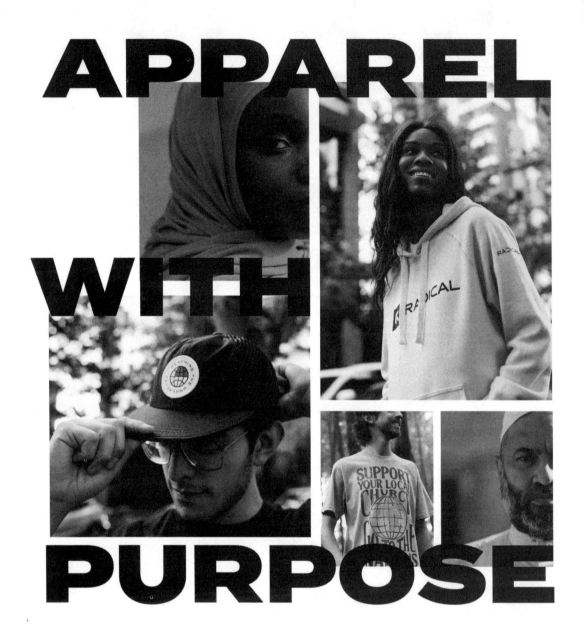

100% of the proceeds from your purchase
go to reaching the unreached

shop.radical.net